MW01289629

A Better Practices Guide for Populating a CMDB - Examples of IT Configuration Management for the Computer Room, the Datacentre and the Cloud

1st Edition, March 2014

Contents

Chapter 1

Introduction

I don't think anyone can write a best practices guide for ITIL configuration management yet, but I've seen some of my clients establish practices that do seem to work quite well.

I have also tried to avoid glossing over anything. Too many guides don't go into any detail, leaving organisations to reinvent the wheel and make the same mistakes.

My goal in this guide, though is not to be prescriptive. I have tried to provide both examples of what my customers have done and also why it worked for them.

There are two kinds of examples in this book:

- Examples relating to well-known commercial products that are in such common use that it makes sense to map exactly what they are like.

- Examples based on my customer's environments. Because of non-disclosure, these have all been anonymised, but I've found that using generic names often makes it easier for customer to map these examples into their environment.

1.1 Why are we doing this?

From what I've seen the clearest benefits of developing a configuration management database (often abbreviated to CMDB or CMS) I've seen have been around:

- Implementing business requirements around who can call the service desk and what response they should expect to receive.

- Reporting, particularly collecting A-vs-B data.

- Being able to express what a change will affect and (more importantly) why a back-out plan hasn't left anything out.

- Precisely defining what a known error refers to.

- Identifying single points of failure and the implications of this for incident management.

- As a filing place for storing documents that you otherwise might have put somewhere else. (e.g. licensing info, vendor management, as-built documentation).

Almost all of my customers use HP Service Manager so many of the examples in this guide refer to functionality in that product, but hopefully you will find that nothing here is overly vendor specific.

Chapter 2

High-level Services

This chapter describes some quick and simple techniques for identifying what services might be worth including in your CMDB.

If you are only interested in the first of the expected benefits from having a CMDB (an implementation of the business requirements around who can call the service desk and what response they should expect to receive), then this may be the only chapter relevant to you. In the next chapter we will show how you can even do some quite valuable reporting.

If you are expecting other business benefits from your CMDB, then you will probably want to map out these high-level services anyway, and I hope you find these techniques helpful in doing this.

2.1 The 15-second CMDB

Customers using HP Service Manager have to have some kind of configuration management database set up. This is because there is a table called "Subscriptions" which maps departments and individuals to business services. This enables the service desk to identify whether or not the caller can legitimately raise a ticket about the matter at hand.

Many organisations stumble at this point and engage in long and lengthy projects to create a configuration database, before even the 1st service call can be raised.

This isn't necessary. All that is absolutely required is a service against which to log calls. If your goal is to support a service desk or incident ticket tracking system and you have been tasked with creating a CMDB to support this, then spend 15 seconds identifying the answer to this question:

What does the organisation call their IT department?

The answer will often be something simple like "IT". So if you can only spend 15 seconds creating a CMDB, create it with just one business service called "IT" – and nothing else. You will then need to create a subscription that says that everyone in the organisation can call about "IT" problems, but you will then be the proud owner of a usable CMDB.

Most small organisations can manage quite adequately with the 15-second CMDB. They often use programs like BestPractical's Request Tracker (rt) for their incident management and change management processes.

2.2 Mapping by Negation

A surprisingly effective way of mapping out some additional business services is with the process I call "mapping by negation". It starts with a simple question:

Is there anyone in the organisation who should *not* be able to call up the service desk about something?

Here are a few examples:

- Two of my customers have both Microsoft Exchange and Lotus Notes. As a Google Apps reseller, this is particularly painful for me to see! Users who have Microsoft Outlook on their computer should not be calling about Lotus Notes, and vice versa.

- A trading company I worked with don't allow junior traders to call up about the trading system until they have completed their training and met some other requirements. If they haven't been given authorisation by the organisation to use the trading system, then the service desk absolutely should not be helping them do anything on it.

- An outsourcing company I did some training for in New Zealand had several clients. Some of the clients had outsourced just the management of the network, other clients had outsourced support for everything including desktops.

In each case there is a service which is supported independently of the others. In HP Service Manager this corresponds to a service which is not subscribed to by a department, or which is subscribed to individually instead of departmentally.

In the first example, an appropriate way to handle this is to have a create a service in the CMDB called "Email (Outlook)" and another service called "Email (Lotus)". While there is a danger of mixing a Technical Service with a Business Service, as long as the business itself doesn't mind this is not really an issue. The departments using Exchange can have subscriptions to the "Email (Outlook)" service which means that their staff can call the service desk and have a call logged in their name correctly; likewise the other departments can have subscriptions to "Email (Lotus)".

In the second example, the trading system was associated with a business service and when an individual met all the requirements to have access to it, a subscription was added to their account which permitted them to call the service desk.

In the final example, the outsourcing company had a number of business services corresponding to the way that sales contracts were drawn up. For each chunk of service that you could buy from the outsourcer, there was a business service. Each customer (who might consist of several departments) was then subscribed to the appropriate business services as per their contract.

2.3   Mapping by support response

Another surprisingly effective way of identifying what should be marked as a service in the CMDB is by looking at differences in support expectations. A handle for identifying this is to ask the following questions:

> **What is *not* urgent? What things could somebody call up about where the appropriate response could be we'll look at tomorrow"?**

I find that this line of questioning is very informative, because it will highlight what absolutely cannot be put off until tomorrow. Both the cannot-be-put-off and the can-be-pushed-off answers are very likely to correspond to services that IT supplies to the business.

There is a related question which asks if there is any individual who should get special treatment for anything in particular. This isn't trying to identify that the CEO expects a fast response across the board, but that the warehouse manager always needs a fast response for calls related to the warehouse management application. Clearly the warehouse management application and its associated components constitute a business service. In HP Service Manager this would be implemented by an individual subscription from the warehouse manager to the warehousing service where a service level agreement is in place which provides for fast response times to calls.

2.4 Mapping by support groups

This method is the most popular, but it tends to generate lots of technical services and very few business services. Essentially this method is to ask a question of each IT team leader:

What do clients ask for support from you?

The reason it doesn't produce very good results is that the answer is often to do with the specific technology: Oracle, Active Directory, PeopleSoft. When you have a business service which depends on the functioning of several different components the language that the business uses won't necessarily match up with the vocabulary of the IT staff.

2.5 Automated techniques

In reality there are no techniques for fully automating the identification of business and technical services. But as artificial intelligence techniques and document processing technologies improve over the next few years it's possible we might see the progress here. (There are of course techniques for mapping out the lower layers of the CMDB very easily, as discussed later.)

The general idea behind these techniques is to analyse large numbers of documents (such as vendor delivered handover documentation, support notes, internal wikis, workshop minutes and so on) and support tickets (usually interaction, incidents and change tickets) looking for words and phrases that are unusual. For example proper nouns which don't correspond to names or places, words that are consistently written in full capital letters and other such cues. These words and phrases often correspond to the way that the business refers to the service.

In practice the technology is not quite there yet. If there is some other justification for implementing an automated tool (for example, Queckt uses these sorts of techniques in order to route tickets to the right team faster) then it may be a useful boost for mapping out services and their relationships.

2.6 Why you could stop here

In this section I will give a few examples of incomplete CMDBs – that had barely more than what you would have developed from the previous chapter – that still provided a lot of value to their owners.

2.6.1 The cable company

I had a student on one of my courses who worked for a cable television and cable Internet company in Australia. We happened to talk about their services model and my student enthusiastically described what their model looked like and how incredibly effective it had been. For each region it looked somewhat like this:

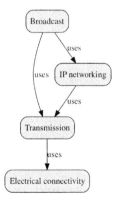

I was surprised but my student observed that the most important services – where essentially all the revenue came from – were broadcast (pay TV) and networking (cable internet). Other internal IT services were not as crucial because they could recover from an outage with a backlog of work to do. All the revenue-servicing teams could relate how they supported one of those four services.

He said that setting up this very basic CMDB had repaid itself many times over by making it very clear what the root cause of outages were. Prior to that they would regularly have broadcast engineers wasting time troubleshooting a problem that was already known and being worked up by the electrical connectivity teams.

It turned out that change management was already a very well established process. Each service layer and well-defined rules about notification and planning changes that could affect another layer.

No one could see any benefit in having deeper insight into the other layers, and in fact there were advantages around audibility to keep strong walls in place to block visibility further.

2.6.2   A vs B Testing

A common practice in large-scale software development is "A vs B" reporting. This is where the developers will tag a small sample of users and give them a slightly different experience. If we put the signup button at the top of the page, do we get more signups? Google once famously performed A versus B testing on different colour shades on a page to see how the user base behave differently in the presence of differ-ent colours!

This can be done in Service Management as well. Not many IT organisations can trial a device or program on a million users, but even samples as small as 25 can produce statistically useful information.

For example, based on past incidents, interactions, problems and outages, should we use Windows or Linux? Should we buy HP or Dell?

To make this happen you need at least two models for one subtype of CI, many occurrences of that CI, some guess at the cost of an incident, interaction and problem and at least a vague measure of the cost of an outage. Also, if there is a significant price difference between the models (e.g. you are comparing iPhones to Nokias) then don't forget to include that in the report as well.

Note that very often this *does not need the individual CI to be identified.* Plan ahead what "A vs B" reporting you plan to do; the service desk only needs to record "A" or "B" as the CI data for you to do this. For ex-ample, if you want to compare laptop vendors, then get the service desk to complete "Affected CI" with "HP Laptops, "Dell Laptops, "Apple Laptops" or "Other Lap-tops". This doesn't take long (it's far faster than getting a user to give a laptop name or serial number) and you can still derive a lot of value from it.

2.6.3 Trend reporting on hardware

The other kind of reporting which can be valuable is a trend on outages (and interactions, incidents and problems). Are systems getting worse over time?

It's often said (usually with great conviction) that some vendor's laptops don't have the same build quality and reliability that they had in the past.

This kind of reporting can be done even if you don't have each laptop recorded individually in your CMDB. Similarly to "A vs B" testing, as long as there is some generic configuration item in the database for the service desk (and other IT staff to use) – such as "Dell Laptops" or "Apple Laptops" – there is enough data to work with.

Be aware that both software and hardware tend to have U-shaped graphs of issues over time – they start out with many issues, become better and eventually end up with so many issues that they are finally disposed of.

This means that if you start recording incidents against a vendorspecific CI today you will almost definitely see more incidents in the future then you're experiencing right now. Why is that? Because you won't be including the faults in the laptops that have been returned as defective in the weeks and months leading up until today since your last major refresh. However, you can use this to compare trends between vendors if you buy from each at similar times.

Chapter 3

Lower-level services

3.1 Automatic Identification

It is possible to discover computers, networking devices and software automatically. There are many software tools that can be used for this.

3.1.1 Brute force with nmap

The most brute force approach is demonstrated in an open source tool called **nmap**. The way nmap works is this: you give it a range of IP addresses that correspond to all your internal networks. It will then attempt to connect to every single one of those addresses, first with a lightweight ping packet, and then by making connections on standard port numbers. Finally, it then sends some very cleverly planned garbage network traffic: it turns out that each different operating system handles this kind of garbage in slightly different ways. So by seeing the response, nmap can take a guess at what version of the operating system is there. Put together, this identifies anything that is connected to a network and what services it offers over the network.

nmap will fail sometimes if there is a firewall blocking traffic to a network. It also has problems sweeping a network which does not run the current generation Internet protocol. (I have only seen a handful of small networks running only IPV6 – the next generation Internet protocol – so this is unlikely to affect discovery in any normal corporate environment.)

3.1.2   Network Node Manager

HP Network Node Manager takes a slightly more sophisticated approach. There is a protocol called the Simple Network Management Protocol (SNMP) which is normally used by network administrators to monitor switches and routers. One of the capabilities of SNMP is that it can query a network device and ask it what other network devices it has recently communicated with. Since nearly every device in any corporate network is either connected to a switch or is communicating with a whilst network base station, and each of these is communicating regularly with an on-site router, querying a few routers will pretty quickly populate a complete database of every device in the organisation. Prior to version 8, HP Network Node Manager used to discover every computer in the network in this way; from version 8 onwards it only discovers switches, routers, wireless base stations and other such low-level networking equipment.

3.1.3 DDM*

Essentially combining the two approaches, HP's DDM products do sweeps (like nmap) and SNMP polling, but then do something even more sophisticated. Having discovered what operating system is being run on a newly discovered device, it will try to install some special software there. This software will then examine every single file on the computer and compare each against a centralised database of programs. If it finds a match (for example, if it finds exactly the right combination of bytes from the Firefox binary) it will record automatically that there is a program called Firefox on the computer.

3.1.4 Limitations

These are very fast and effective ways of populating CMDB, but in the deluge of data created the most important information is still missing. It's possible to identify that Firefox is installed on all the computers in the payroll office; analysis of network traffic could identify that Firefox is being used to connect to the PeopleSoft payroll application, but it will not say why they are doing this and whether there is any alternative. That is, if Firefox stopped working for some reason, could the payroll staff switch to using Internet Explorer instead?

Quite often there are limitations in the even rudimentary analysis done by automated tools. Identification of clustered applications is often very weak and if you have a custom written in-house application most tools will be able to do little more than identify what computers it is running on.

Ultimately there is still a need at the moment for manual recording of relationships between configurations items, and in many cases the need for manual creation of congressional items. As this is the most expensive and time-consuming part of creating a CMDB, this is where it is most important to be sure that there is some business value in what you're doing.

3.2   Outage propagation

The first step is to configure your service management application to track outages and to propagate them to related configuration items.

3.2.1   Enable global propagation in HP Service Manager

The following screenshot shows how to do this in HP Service Manager. It is found in the service level agreement administration section in the menu concerned with availability level agreements. Firstly there is a checkbox called "Spread Outages" which enables the propagation of incidents. The second checkbox ("Extend outage spreading to more than one level") is essential for modelling complex applications because the model operates across many different levels.

Put together, it now means that when a technical support engineer marks a configuration item as being down, if that had ramifications on other configuration items, the other items will be marked as down as well. This is particularly effective when combined with a monitoring system which automatically generate incidents in HP Service Manager.

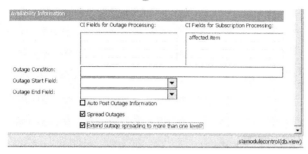

3.2.2 Per-relationship configuration in HP Service Manager

The next step is to configure for each relationship what is required in order for a cascade of the outage to occur. The next screenshot shows how this is done in HP Service Manager. This is the screen that you will see when you create or modify a relationship between two configuration items. If the "Outage Dependency" tick box is enabled then the greyed-out box below it becomes active and you can choose any number from 1 upwards.

Chapter 4

Inside the Organisation

There are some differences between the kind of information you need to maintain in a CMDB for applications and services that are developed and implemented in-house, versus applications and services that are either partly or wholly run in the cloud.

In this chapter we will be looking at two extremes for in-house applications: the very small and simple, and the very large and complex. Finally we'll talk about modelling databases.

4.1   LAMP applications

LAMP is an acronym for Linux, Apache, MySQL, PHP. These are 4 open source (free) technologies that have been very popular for developing simple web applications since the late 1990s. Over time the meaning has shifted: instead of PHP, the P can also stand for other common succinct programming languages such as Perl or Python; and instead of the MySQL database, PostgreSQL has become more popular; and finally, alternate free operating systems such as FreeBSD and OpenBSD are sometimes used in place of Linux.

Traditionally, this style of application development became very popular because of its low resource requirements. Even a second-hand computer that would otherwise be thrown out because was unusually slow is often fast enough to run the kinds of simple web applications which LAMP is famous for.

Nowadays LAMP applications tend to be found performing important but not mission-critical applications, and instead of being installed onto an old computer way run inside virtual machines where there low resource consumption means of they can coexist with other applications are easily.

Sometimes LAMP applications grow up and become mission-critical. Then, instead of running all on a single machine, they end up with multiple front-end web servers running the PHP component, and often some sort of database replication mechanism. Essentially they turn into something that looks very much like a modern enterprise application (discussed in its own chapter).

One of the most interesting observations about this is that there is a period of transition were they move from being stand-alone, isolated, unimportant applications to being highly redundant, protected important applications and during this period there are often major mismatches between the reliance that the business has upon the application and the level of support that the IT organisation can supply.

This is one of the times that good CMDB models can be extremely valuable.

4.1.1 Naive (and unhelpful) modelling of LAMP applications

LAMP autodiscovery is very hard. It is quite easy to discover that a particular computer is installed with Linux; checking to see that it runs Apache is also easy (by connecting to TCP port 80, or by running the rpm or dpkg commands to see what is installed); seeing that PHP is a configured module of Apache can also be automated; identifying that MySQL drivers are included in PHP is also easy (run "php -v").

Where it gets difficult is working out which PHP files correspond to which application. It's very unlikely that any auto discovery tool would have the signatures of any in-house PHP applications.

Even tier 1 supported and very famous applications are often not in autodiscovery tool signature databases. For example the world's leading e-learning learning management system (LMS) is a LAMP application called Moodle. Even though it is widely in use in large enterprises, I'm yet to see it automatically get discovered by any tool.

It gets more difficult: often the database connection information is hardcoded into the PHP program. This alters the signature of the file to make it unique in the world. It also makes it very hard for any discovery tool to identify which database instance is being contacted by the application.

It may get even more difficult still as there is no guarantee that the existence of PHP module in Apache server is actually getting used. It could well be that the application running on the computer is actually written in Python or Perl. In almost every case there will be some kind of application framework (Symphony, Cakewalk, Mason or Django) in which the application sits as well.

Because of all these issues, it's not uncommon to see CMDB models of LAMP applications which look like the following:

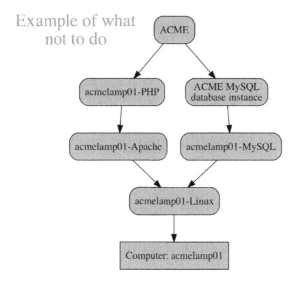

There are a number of problems with this model. Firstly, it provides very little additional value. What does it mean for there to be a fault on the PHP component? How would we distinguish that from a fault in the ACME application or fault in Apache?

Secondly, it introduces needless complexity and a large number of configuration items to be supported. When an administrator raises a change request to do a point upgrade of a fundamental library (the equivalent of Windows patches for the operating system) they will have to raise it against 3 configuration items: PHP, Apache and Linux.

Lastly almost every component is going to be supported by the same team. I've never seen an organisation where PHP, Apache and Linux weren't all managed by the same UNIX administration team. I have seen situations where MySQL is administered by database team, but even that is unusual and quite often MySQL is administered by the same UNIX administration team that looks after the rest of the stack. (Usually they perform some kind of support for the PHP applications themselves before passing it back to whoever it was that developed it; but quite often some of the simpler PHP applications yet written by the administration team themselves.)

4.1.2   A better model

This following diagram is often a more useful way of modelling a LAMP application in the CMDB.

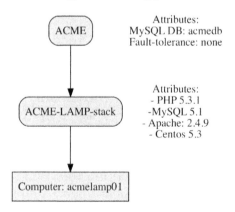

The main advantage of the model is that it shows **substitutability**. A sadly all too common scenario is that a large company has bought a number of small companies and a LAMP application acquired in that process runs perfectly for several months and then fails. Quite often there is another server that could be used very quickly and easily (because it has similar versions of PHP, MySQL and Apache), but finding it is often tricky. Even rebuilding can sometimes be challenging if the required versions aren't documented somewhere convenient.

By creating a special Software subclass (LAMP-stack), the CMDB can very clearly reflect what is being used. Note also that all the attributes of the LAMP-stack CI can be automatically discovered, including which computer they are running on.

The only part that cannot be discovered automatically is in fact the top level and its attributes. If the database is actually running on a different host, then it might make sense to create a dependency from the ACME application to the database, but if it is running locally (as it often is) it will probably be administered by the same team and have the same incident outage propagation as the other components in the LAMP-stack.

One important attribute to include is how fault-tolerant the setup is. In an ideal world of course everything would be fault tolerant and no single point of failure could cause an application to fail. In reality this is often too expensive to implement, particularly for second-tier applications which are not part of the bottleneck workflow of the organisation. (See Eliyahu Goldratt's *Theory of Constraints* for more information about why money spent fixing one part of the organisation can sometimes actually be detrimental overall.)

Some practice, we often have to make do and not give applications the best infrastructure.

I like to use this 4 category selection to describe the fault-tolerant status of a LAMP application:

- **None**. The entire stack runs on a single PC with no disk mirroring or other kind of hardware protection. I hope you have a good backup!

- **Data-protected**. The entire stack runs on a single PC which has some kind of disk mirroring or RAID protection. This will still need good backups.

- **Data-replicated**. The entire stack might be running on a single PC, or perhaps the database server is on a different computer. Some kind of log shipping or replication of the internal database (and any supporting data files) is being done. In this case while a single failure could take the application off-line, the data would still be available to use when the application is started again.

- **Hardware fault protected**. The entire stack runs on a virtual machine which can be switched to another hosting server transparently. No single hardware failure can cause the application to become off-line, nor can any single hardware failure cause data to be lost.

It is possible to have higher levels of full tolerance (for example by running more than one web server and by running active clustered databases) but in those cases, essentially the model is like a modern enterprise application and should be modelled as such.

4.2 Modern enterprise applications

Modern enterprise applications are web-based and written to avoid having any single points of failure. In other words, if a computer or device crashes end users won't notice this happening. They will continue to interact with their web browser, and the infrastructure will make sure that their session carries on without interruption.

Modern enterprise applications generally consist of:

- A load balancer
- A web tier
- An application tier
- A database

The published URL – the one that users click on to start the application – will often correspond to the IP address of a **front end load balancer**. This is a confusing name, because there usually isn't a single device performing the load balancing. The load balancer usually consists of several routers. There will be a section of the internal configuration of these routers which says what IP address to listen on for incoming connections, and which web front end to relay those connections onto. Every few seconds they will check to make sure which web front ends are alive, and remember which did not respond so as not to forward any connections onto them.

In your organisation these load balancers may be supported by the network administration team (if the load balancers are running on Cisco equipment for example) or perhaps by a UNIX administration team (if the load balancers are running on OpenBSD, which is a highly secure version of UNIX).

The **web front ends** are usually Java programs packaged as a "war" (web archive) file. Quite often, the war file is something that no discovery program has been trained to recognise.

Often this is because they are written in-house, but even commercially-distributed applications are often not in application discovery databases: they are rare, hard to get hold of, and sometimes personalised per customer. Even if the discovery program does recognise the war file, the war file is actually expanded into many independent files when the web application server starts up, and often customised to say which application server to connect to. Very few discovery programs cope with this well.

There will be at least two **web servers**, which run the web front ends. There will possibly be more depending on how big the application is and how heavily used it is. These web servers are often Linux servers because they are cheap, or otherwise Windows or occasionally Solaris. These web serving farms often run the front ends for several enterprise applications. Depending on what is entered by the user in their web browser, they will choose which web front end to execute.

The web front end simply re-formulates and displays results which were returned by the actual **application engines** which are running on **application server** farm. Sometimes these application servers are shared between different enterprise applications, and sometimes each server is dedicated to its task. These are often much larger, more expensive servers than web servers. Often there will be many more application servers than web servers depending on the complexity of the application. There will almost always be more than one application server, so that if one crashes the others carry on. The web tier generally has some way of knowing which application servers are running, or at least they know to retry failed connections to another application server.

The application engines are structured similarly to the web application and will have a Java program running on them, packaged up as a war file that is expanded as soon as the application server starts. Again the shrapnel of the war file expansion will often be customised, usually to indicate which database to connect to.

I will talk about modelling of **databases** in a later section.

4.2.1 The web-tier

Suppose you have been asked to model the ACME application. ACME depends on the load balancing configured for the ACME application: if that load balancing service is not working then users will not be able to get to the application at all. So this is a dependency where if one component is down, the whole is down.

The load balancing configuration for the ACME application will rely on the web front end to be working. Again if the web front-end infrastructure is down then the ACME load balancing will be down, which will imply that the ACME application is down. So there's a "down if one item is down" dependency there as well.

Let's assume that there are just two web front ends for ACME and that they are running on the first two web servers in the organisation. The "ACME web front ends" service will depend on web front-end 1 and web front-end to, but it would only be considered down if both front ends were down, because it can still continue to operate cleanly and correctly with only one working web front end. Therefore, the relationship is entered as propagating "down" only if *two* supporting configuration items are down.

Obviously if the web server on which a web front end was supposed to be running is down, then that web front-end is down. So this is a typical "down if one item is down" dependency.

Here is the whole model, highlighting the configuration items mentioned in the previous paragraphs.

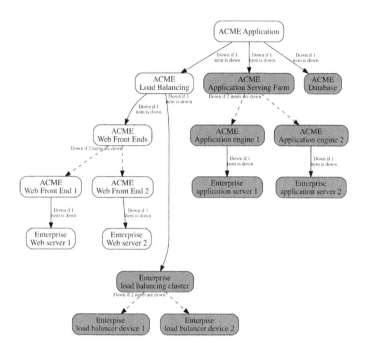

4.2.2 Load balancing

Moving on to the next diagram highlighting the load balancing part, the ACME load balancing configuration obviously also depends on the hardware in use in the organisation for load balancing. We wouldn't want to have the ACME load balancing service depend directly on the pair of enterprise load balancing devices because it will become painful to maintain this model in the future as load balancers get replaced. By having the ACME load balancer service depend on the enterprise load balancing *cluster* we can later add and remove devices and only need to update one set of relationships (the relationship between the enterprise load balancing cluster and the modified device).

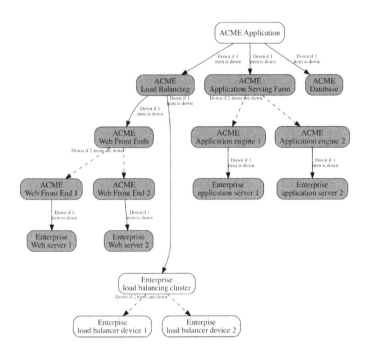

4.2.3 Application Engines

Finally, the application engines are modelled. Since the application service itself can survive and continue to operate even when one application engine is unavailable, there is a "down if two items are down" dependency between the application serving farm and the application engines.

In this case it is not quite so clear cut that there needs to be an application serving farm configuration item. We could have had the ACME application depend directly on the application engines. The best reason not to do this is that it is likely that you will have a monitoring system which can report on the status of the whole farm as well as individual engines. It is more convenient for this monitoring system to be able to generate incidents recorded against the whole serving farm rather than having to modify the monitoring system to list all application engines any incident that it creates.

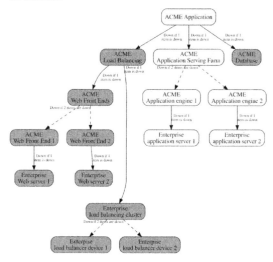

4.2.4 Summary

In summary the following diagram shows what the model is likely to look like. Note that there will be other configuration items depending on the 2 enterprise web servers; there will be many, many other load balancing services depending on the enterprise load balancing cluster; there may well be other applications depending on the enterprise application servers.

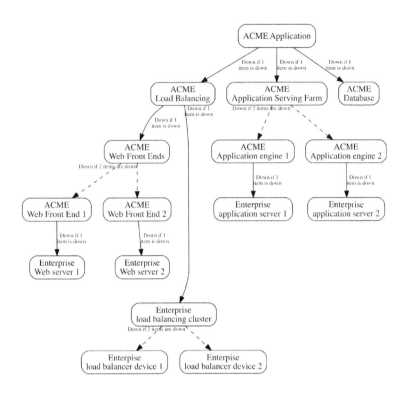

4.3 Databases

Databases are by far the hardest CI's to model. They are also the hardest to do useful change management with.

This section is going to refer to relational databases that use SQL. Examples of this are the free tools MySQL and PostgreSQL; and the commercial tools: Oracle, MS-SQL, Sybase and many others. A later section will talk briefly about some other kinds of databases.

4.3.1 Impacts of failures

To make impact propagation work correctly, it's important to correctly identified the dependencies. The following diagrams illustrate how to do this.

Databases can run stand-alone on a single computer. They can also be running on large numbers of computers in parallel. In the latter case it is important to distinguish between sharded databases and replicated databases.

Database sharding is a technique to deliver better performance out of low-end databases. If you had to maintain a database listing the phone numbers of every English speaker in the world (i.e. a database of roughly 1,000,000,000 entries) and you also needed to be able to look up this database at very high speed (perhaps a few thousand times per second you would likely run into some performance problems. If you discovered that your database could only keep up with around 50 lookups per second you might choose to create 26 independent databases, each of which contained entries for people whose name began with each letter of the alphabet. You would have created a sharded database consisting of 26 independent databases.

In this example the sharded database is now 26 times more likely to fail because if any individual database failed, the sharded database is likely to become unusable.

The following diagram shows a model for 4-way sharded database. Note that each shard is its own database, and therefore might have redundancy built-in as well.

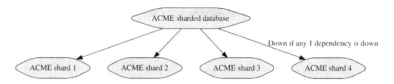

On the other hand, a database which runs in parallel on 2 computers will be much more resilient because the loss of one computer will probably not cause the entire database to fail.

While it is possible to share this kind of part-database role with other functions, it simply isn't done very often. (I saw it once in 2004 on a pair of HP-UX system running MC-Serviceguard to cluster Oracle RAC which also ran HP Operations Manager. The customer redesigned it very soon after going live.)

So there is little harm in ignoring the software layer between the database instance and the computer itself. The impact will be the same.

Some of these parallel databases run "shared nothing" and others share storage. The diagram below shows a share storage solution. Incidents which affect the storage itself (for example the disk array in which the storage exists failing) are recorded against the storage; incidents where a computer is unable to access the storage would be recorded against the computer (because the other computer would be able to continue functioning).

Note that many important attributes (discussed in the next section) have been left off the following diagram.

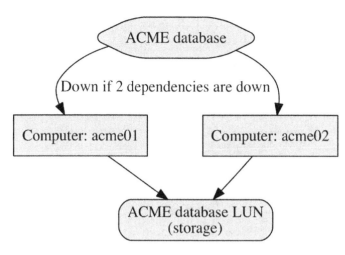

A common feature in almost all databases (SQLite is the only exception that I am aware of) is the ability to do log shipping. This means that whenever a record is updated or added on one computer, that there will be a corresponding update made on another computer. While the second computer may not be able to respond to database queries immediately, there is usually some quite quick procedure for turning the second computer into the master so that any application depending on their database instance can carry on with only a short interruption.

A model for this is quite similar to the parallel model above, but with the added CI for ACME failover. This is included because the failover can have an outage even though the computer may be functioning correctly.

I haven't included storage explicitly in this example because sometimes these log shipping databases are small enough that they are stored on internal disks in the computer. (For example the database might be only 100 MB in size, but still quite valuable. It's unlikely that this would be put onto SAN storage, but would be replicated from internal disk on one computer to the internal disk on another.) Obviously, if you have a dependency on SAN storage in your log shipped database then you would create another two storage CIs (one for each computer).

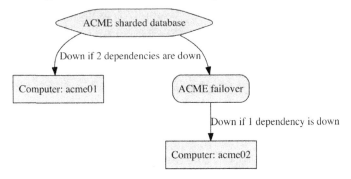

4.3.2   Change Management and Attributes

Change management for databases is very, very hard. It has been described as patching a helicopter in mid-flight.

If you want to make a change to a database, you run a script. There is no backing out short of restoring the database, backup. You can run another script which might undo the effect of the first script, but you can't run that first script in reverse.

Therefore, the best practices around change management for databases is to have a change script library. Each item in this change script library will have:

- **A unique id**. This unique id only has to be unique for the database; if two different databases happen to use the same numbering scheme for their change script libraries it wouldn't matter much.

- **The name of the application** (database) which it targets.

- Which **version or release number** of its target application this can be applied on to.

- Running this script may cause the database to be compatible with another version or release number of the application. If so, **which one**?

- Some **SQL code** that performs the work, including updating a "database versioning table" so that it is possible to see what has been applied.

- Which **environments** (e.g. just development, test, UAT, etc.) this script has successfully run in.

I do not think that it makes sense for this change script library's contents to be stored as CIs even though each script is a program. What does make sense is for the CI representing each database to have an attribute of what version it is up to. This should match the information in the database versioning table, and it is easy to automate and automatic audit of this. (In HP Service Manager environments, simply update the relevant attribute in UCMDB.)

Obviously, it is also necessary to record what database vendor product and product version this database runs as (for example MS-SQL Server 2012, or Oracle 11g).

But other than this I have not seen many other important attributes. Code page and locale can be important because some backup tools can't restore to different locale or code page. Some applications also have problems dealing with different code pages and locales. But most organisations have this quite well standardised with every database identical.

4.3.3   Something odd to look out for

It's quite common for an extract-transform-load (ETL) application to write to a database which is also used by an application. A sensible way to model this is for the database to have a dependency on the ETL which loads data into it; the ETL would have a dependency on the databases and data sources that it reads from.

The following diagram shows this but also something slightly odd. It shows two applications accessing the same database. Most definitely, this does happen in real IT organisations and it is a kind of warning sign.

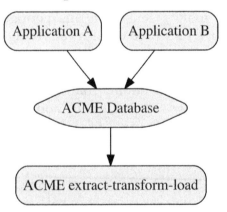

Normally the correct way for two applications to talk to the same database is if there is some kind of broker application in between. Sometimes this is called an enterprise services bus (ESB); sometimes there is a web services interface; on older applications they may be some kind of command-line interface to call. The reason for this is that it minimises the amount of testing needed for a change to be deployed if there is a wrapper to isolate impacts.

If two applications talk directly to the same database, then it is possible that a change to the database to support new functionality in application A may have some unexpected impact on application B. In fact, seeing the Warning-V (as I call it) is a very good predictor of change failure in changes for both of the applications and for the database itself.

4.3.4 Other types of database

There are some other database models, which need to be handled differently.

- There are applications whose database just consists of files in a filesystem. I can't see any reason why these would need to be included in a CMDB model: administration will be performed by the team that runs the application or the underlying server; there would be no way to distinguish between a failure in the file system and failure in the application, so ticket assignment is irrelevant; and change management could simply use the application object to store any attributes under management.

- There are many NoSQL databases. NoSQL is the generic name to cover databases that use some other model other than traditional SQL structures.

The term came into use as companies delivering webpages to millions of users hit upon some of the performance limitations forced by maintaining internal consistency and atomicity from traditional database solutions. Examples include memcache (which does not store anything long-term and only uses memory), Hadoop / HBase, CouchDB and many others. Each is so varied is nearly impossible to say anything meaningful about modelling them in general.

Chapter 5

In the Cloud

There are essentially 3 kinds of cloud delivered service.

- Software as a service

- Platform as a service

- Infrastructure as a service

Each of these have very different requirements in the CMDB.

5.1 Software-as-a-service

Of the more common models for cloud hosted applications is where the supplier provides the application (usually as a website) and takes full administrative control over it. Examples are: Google Apps, Saasu and Xero (web-based accounting applications), Salesforce and many others.

The models for these kinds of applications are very simple. Very often you would include the name of the Saas (software as a service) application in your CMDB as a business service, a technical service or as software. It doesn't particularly matter which. You are primarily doing this so that you can record service desk requests against a relevant configuration item.

Incident and problem tickets will usually be little more than placeholders in your system to record the reference number of the corresponding ticket you received from the vendor.

You will probably still want to raise change tickets against the configuration item representing this Saas application. For example if you were turning on mandatory 2 factor authentication in Google apps, you would want to go through the normal change process that use. There would be some kind of testing done where you confirmed on a subdomain that it was safe to do so; they would be an approval process to make sure that no one was going to be unduly affected by this; and you would have a scheduled date for when you brought it across the organisation. But there is probably little point in storing an attribute for 2-factor authentication status in the CMDB because there is no way of validating what it is set to without a lot of development effort, there is a log in the Google Apps admin console that tracks when it actually was changed (and by whom), and the attribute may be changed in meaning or existence by Google at any time.

5.1.1 Google Apps in detail

Taking the Google Apps example a little further, if you absolutely wanted to split the model for Google Apps further, it is possible to do so. As of March 2014, Google Apps consists of a small number of independent components, with a very flat hierarchy.

To be complete, you would then need to create a very simple monitoring system which regularly polled the Google status page (http://www.google.com/appsstatus) and depending on what it found there, marked the appropriate subservice as down. Each configuration item needs to have a support team (assignment group), but the lower levels would only have placeholders as only Google have the rights to make any changes there.

Most Saas solutions look like this – a very flat hierarchy with little visibility.

5.2 Platform-as-a-service

PaaS is the least common cloud model. Essentially, a vendor takes the shared components from the architecture of modern web apps and rents them out. The customer uploads war files (or their equivalents) and the vendor runs those applications for them.

The most popular PaaS provider is Google App Engine,

which has essentially nothing in common with Google Apps despite its name. HP's public cloud has an equivalent (called Stackato) and Amazon has a service for running Java applications. Other PaaS providers include Heroku (who specialise in running programs written in Ruby).

Unsurprisingly, CMDB models for applications running a PaaS look like a mixture of a modern web application and a SaaS solution. However, there are some important differences.

5.2.1   Multiple live versions

In order to differentiate their offerings from doing it yourself on infrastructure as a service (see next chapter), the sophistication of the PaaS providers' infrastructure is often quite remarkable. For example, a feature which is present in nearly every PaaS provider is that of traffic splitting. You don't want to roll out a new version of the application and have thousands of customers affected all once, so traffic splitting lets you choose a tiny subset and trial out the new version on those customers while keeping existing customers on the previous version. If no problems come to light then you start bringing in a few more customers to use the new version, and then a few more, and so on until you have migrated everybody to the new version.

This kind of rolling, live upgrade is not common in any other style of application. This means that setting up the CMDB to define these kinds of services requires special care.

For example, when a user or customer contacts the service desk because they are expressing an issue with a PaaS delivered application, the service desk will almost definitely not know which version is actually being interacted with. (If the service desk have tools so that they can find out this information quickly, all the better.) So you will always need to have a configuration item representing an unknown version of the application.

When a technical person investigates a ticket for a "unknown version" configuration item, the first activity they will do is to identify which version that user is interacting with. They will then update the ticket setting the "Affected CI" to the appropriate version of the application.

Some CMDB administrators find this very weird. They consider version to be simply an attribute of a configuration item; when there is an upgrade the change record updates the version. They find something odd in the idea that you will create several different CIs, one for each version (plus an "unknown version") and that each CI might only have a lifespan of weeks, or possibly days.

5.2.2 Multiple live modules

Google App Engine breaks encourages developers to break down applications into even smaller chunks than other development environments generally do. Many applications out therefore broken up into modules; each module can have multiple versions deployed. Each module will generally have an associated CI in the CMDB as well. Again, when there is an issue, it may not be immediately apparent which version of a module the issue relates to, so having an "unknown version" for each module can be useful to initially record a ticket against.

5.2.3   An example CMDB model

There will be an over-arching technical service or application under which everything else sits.

The remaining components can be modelled as dependencies, but I have not found any occasion in which impact calculations work. Firstly, the PaaS applications have such extraordinary redundancy built-in, that an outage requires an even more extraordinary disaster to have any effect. Secondly, the most common form of failure (which is extremely rare) is the PaaS platform itself. This is out of the control of anyone except for the vendor. The left-over impacts are so obscure and infrequent that the impact modelling will almost never be cost-effective to do.

There will always be a "core" module – the one that handles the top-level URL. Usually, there will be versioned modules as well. This means that a typical CMDB model for an application which runs in a PaaS environment will look like this:

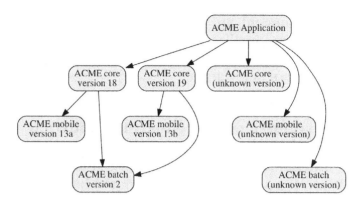

In this diagram, the developers of the ACME application have currently deployed version 18 and version 19 of the core module. They may be using traffic splitting to send some trial users to version 19. There is a module for handling the application's mobile (small-screen) interface as well. There are two versions of this, 13a and 13b (versions do not have to be numeric) which are currently live. They happen to be used by version 18 and version 19 of the application respectively. There is also some kind of batch back-end (for example, a long-running job for running data analytics) which is called by both version 18 and version 19.

5.2.4 What we don't have in the CMDB

Notice also that some relationships that are important for in-house applications are completely missing in the CMDB models for PaaS-delivered applications. How many instances (copies) of this program running? On what computers are they running? In a typical PaaS environment this information isn't easily accessible, changes all the time and is of no relevance anyway.

Many of the CI attributes of an application running

in PaaS environment are also quite unusual. In the next two sections I will highlight the most important of these attributes which are not commonly found in any other kind of application.

5.2.5   Attributes of the top-level application

- **Admin users**. Who are the authorised users who can deploy new versions, perform roll-backs and look at logs? This information is usually available in the PaaS platform console, but generally only available to other admin users. If it's 2am in the morning and there's an urgent need for an operator to find someone, being able to find this information in the CMDB can sometimes be valuable enough to pay for a large chunk of the CMDB development cost!

- **Currently serving version numbers**. When a change ticket is raised to alter a traffic splitting policy or to start sending traffic to a previously-unused version, the change ticket should include a CMDB attribute update for the what versions are being served.

- **Data stores**. While it is possible to model the back-end storage services (e.g. the built-in data-store, a relational database such as mysql, a binary object store), the PaaS vendor is the only one who can perform administrative functions on them, or to fix them when they break. So I include what sort of data storage the application uses simply as a plain-text attribute; it is useful to have it conveniently referenced for data cost planning and data consolidation, but it is not used for much else other than that.

5.2.6 Attributes of each underlying application and module version

- **Software version control tag**: A PaaS delivered application is likely to be being developed quite rapidly. Each version that is deployed should correspond to a particular check out of the source code to the application. Any sensible programmers will keep their source code in a version control system (subversion and git are very common choices). Software version control systems can keep track of significant checkouts by tagging it with a release code. This release code tag may be as prosaic as VERSION_18 or it might have a name such as DORAEMON. Whatever the tag was, it needs to be recorded as an attribute of the CI for this version of the application in the CMDB.

- **PaaS environment version**: The PaaS vendors are constantly upgrading their environments and adding extra capabilities, and sometimes obsoleting functionality. Generally what happens is that there is a version of the environment to which the application was deployed which supplies the functionality that it needs and was written specifically for. Because of this, there is often a very tight coupling between the version of the application and a version of the underlying environment. For example, version 18 of the application may be written to run with version 1.4 of theP-aaS environment, and version 19 may be written to run with version 1.5. Keeping track of this is crucially important for root cause analysis and known error tracking. So every CI representing a PaaS hosted application should record the PaaS environment version.

- **Experimental APIs in use**. When a PaaS provider develops a new subsystem, though often deploy it in phases: firstly a limited preview which is available to invited customers; then a preview available to customers who choose to opt-in; then a longer period where it is available to everyone but still marked as experimental; and finally frozen and supported as an interface which can be relied on for production applications. In any phase prior to last one, the interface which programs use to interact with that subsystem may be subject to change. Unfortunately, it is sometimes necessary for programs to go live and be in production and be depending to some extent on application programming interfaces (APIs) which are not in that final phase where they can be relied upon. Thus it's very important to flag which experimental APIs are in use in each version of the deployed application and/or module. This makes troubleshooting issues related to the changes in these APIs much easier.

5.3   Infrastructure as a Service

While many ISPs and web hosting companies have offered virtual machines for rent since virtualisation first became possible on commodity platforms, it was after

Amazon started offering their infrastructure for rent by the hour that the idea of infrastructure as a service became mainstream.

Almost every major IT company and a large number of telecommunication companies offer some kind of infrastructure as a service. Here is a very brief list of some of the most common:

- Amazon EC2 (elastic compute cloud)

- HP public cloud

- Google Compute Engine

- Microsoft Azure

- Rackspace

- Rimuhosting

- Cloud 9

In general the way these services work is that they have a selection of disk images (some standard ones, some community created ones, and also the option to create them yourself). Either through a web console, or through a programming language interface you choose which disk image to use, and how much memory and CPU power you want in a new virtual machine. The vendor's systems then create a virtual machine of the right size to boot from the disk image that you chose.

You then either login to the virtual machine remotely to configure it and install any applications you need, or your special disk image is already configured to run all the programs that you need it to run.

Sometime later (perhaps a few minutes, or perhaps years later) you use the same web interface or programming language interface to shut down that virtual machine. The memory and disk of the virtual machine are then lost.

There is usually also the option of creating persistent storage, which is a disk image which you can attach and detach from any of the virtual machines. Databases or archives are sometimes put onto this kind of persistent storage.

Another common feature is the ability to set up networking and firewalling. When you create a virtual machine, you choose which security group it is to be put into. Each security group has rules which define what connections are allowed in and which are blocked. For example a security group for web servers may allow connections in on port 80 (the port number for ordinary non-secure web traffic); a security group for database servers might allow port 5432 (the port number for ordinary traffic being sent to the PostgreSQL database system).

In some providers you cannot change which security group a machine is in after it has been booted – all you can do is terminate that virtual machine, and start a new one up in the correct security group.

Most infrastructure providers also supply "bucket" storage which is similar to a shared drive in some ways. These buckets are often used for storing log files, application binaries, storage of large files that users have uploaded into an application, backups and any other situation where it's important to have cheap storage that can grow very simply and efficiently.

The above list of services are common to almost all infrastructure as a service providers, but Amazon in particular provides many other services as well, such as DNS (name serving), messaging and queueing, virtual private networks, tape storage, relational databases, data warehousing, monitoring, data processing, search and many other useful functions.

5.3.1 Pets vs Cattle

An analogy which has been used by many writers is that of pets and cattle. In some cultures the same animal species can be used by the same family as both a pet and as a food source. For example, dogs in Vietnam, or Mary and her little lamb. We treat pets differently to cattle: when a pet is sick, we take it to the vet and give it medicine. Pets have names. We record the history of pets and record many events in their lives.

Cattle may receive medicine, and there are situations where a vet may be called to treat cattle, but very often the response to unwell cattle is to terminate. Cattle do not generally have names, although they may have numbers, or other identifying tags. Only the very most important events (birth, death and a few others) are recorded.

The same is true of virtual machines created in IaaS environments. Some of these virtual machines will be treasured, have a clear and definite role and will be kept very carefully under change management. However, the vast majority of virtual machines will be automatically spun up, exist for a period of time and be terminated.

If something goes wrong with a "pet" virtual machine

a system administrator will investigate and tried to repair the problem, possibly by bringing a file back from a backup or perhaps by restarting some programs. If anything goes wrong with a "cattle" virtual machine, it will probably be terminated automatically by some sort of internal monitoring system and respawned from a fresh disk image.

This has significant implications for the practice of CMDB, as discussed in the next two sections.

5.3.2   Pet Virtual Machines

"Pet" virtual machines can be distinguished because:

- Generally, they have hostnames chosen by human being which match some naming convention which also applies to computers in a datacentre.

- Administrators log in to "pet" virtual machines in order to make changes, look at logs, upgrade software and so on.

- They are backed up somehow.

"Pet" virtual machines should be treated no differently to a physical or virtual machine inside a own data centre.

There are a few attributes (all of which can be autodiscovered) to have in the CMDB which are generally not used for an in-datacentre virtual machine.

- **Region**. This will be a special string defining which datacentre the virtual machine was created in. For Amazon, this can be Singapore, us-west-1 and several others. It

- **Security group**. If this virtual machine fails, it will need to be recreated as it was before, and the security group is the most important to get right.

- **Instance size**. Again, if the virtual machine is accidentally deleted, recreating it with the same CPU and memory configuration can be helpful.

- **Persistent disk**. If this virtual machine services an important purpose, its data will be written to a persistent root disk. Recovering should be as simple as booting up a suitable instance of the right size, in the right security group in the right region off the same disk. So while it would be peculiar to capture a boot disk as a CI inside an organisation's datacentre, it can be useful to record this for cloud-hosted infrastructure. If nothing else, the organisation is paying for it.

In-datacentre virtual machines will often have other attributes which aren't relevant. For example, the VMware version of a virtual machine, which Hyper-V cluster it runs on or which SAN it is connected: none of these are relevant to IaaS-hosted systems from most vendors.

5.3.3 Cattle

Conversely "cattle" virtual machines:

- Have the default hostname issued to them by the infrastructure as a service provider

- No one ever logs into them. Software is not upgraded in place: instead the machine is terminated and a new machine with new software is respawned.

- They have no state which needs to be backed up. Even the log files are generally consolidated into some central location.

As a result of this, **"Cattle" virtual machines should not appear in the CMDB**.

The **disk image** from which they are spawned and the scripts that are used for initialising the virtual machine to its intended purpose should be kept in the CMDB instead.

5.3.4   Discovery

Discovery of computers, storage and associated services is much, much easier when using an infrastructure as a service provider than it is inside an organisation's own computer room. After all, you can leave a computer plugged in in a datacentre and have it overlooked, but an infrastructure as a service provider will guarantee that you are billed for everything that you use.

UCMDB does a very good job of discovering infrastructure in the Amazon compute cloud and also in the HP public cloud. However, on neither platform is it able to distinguish between "pet" virtual machines and "cattle" virtual machines.

Also the CIs that are important in a typical application deployed in an IaaS cloud are a little different to what would be important in a traditional datacentre housed application. The next sections discuss this.

5.3.5 Security groups

A security group is the container in which computers run which defines what firewalling rules apply – that is, which services they can connect to. Security groups can be automatically discovered (even though HP UCMDB version 10 does not do this by default). It is useful to have security groups recorded in the CMDB so that applications can be explicitly called out on their security group dependencies. One of the challenges some organisations face is figuring out which security groups are still in use, and what they are in use for. This can be easily documented in the CMDB.

5.3.6 Object buckets

Because object stores are generally the most efficient way of delivering static content (they can be cached well, and most providers include a content delivery network which means they are retrieved from the international site closest to the user requesting the content), images and supporting data files are often stored in buckets.

These buckets can have thousands of items in them, often with a name which may be simply a long hexadecimal string and very obscure content, so it is not always immediately obvious what a bucket is doing.

It is important to know which buckets are still in use and by what applications (both which applications are writing to the buckets and also which applications are causing reads from the buckets).

Object buckets have two attributes that are worth recording (there are several others which are less likely to need to be kept under change management, such as permissions):

- **Name**. Amazon object buckets begin with the string `s3://`

- **Retention policy**. This can be retrieved automatically. The retention policy defines what happens to objects as they age. Do objects get deleted automatically after a month? Do they get archived to tape (e.g. with Amazon Glacier)? Or are they preserved forever. Altering the retention policy is definitely something that you want to keep under change management and to raise incidents about it is changed without authorisation.

5.3.7 Disk images

There are two difference kinds of disk images, both of which should be in the CMDB: block stores, and machine images. Amazon calls these EBS (elastic block store) and Amazon machine images (AMIs). The HP Cloud calls these volumes and images.

A machine image is a template which is stored in very cheap storage. When you create a new virtual machine from a machine image, the machine image is copied onto the local disk area of the invisible computer which is hosting the virtual machine you created as that virtual machine's boot disk.

You can choose instead to make the virtual machine boot from storage held on a SAN in the IaaS provider's infrastructure (also known as a block store). Usually you would do this by creating a virtual machine and specifying to copy the machine image to a block store.

You can also have block stores created and used as disks other than the boot disk.

All these disk options should be tracked in the CMDB. Creating a disk image commits the organisation to spending money every month until the disk image is deleted. This might only be a few cents, but it is a commitment nevertheless. The only exception would be a block store used as the root disk of a "pet" virtual machine. It's hard to come up with a situation where it would be worthwhile tracking that as a different CI to the machine itself. (After all, we don't usually track the boot disk of a physical machine has its own independent CI).

Since "cattle" virtual machines will essentially be identical copies of the same machine image, change management should track attributes of the machine image itself.

The choice of attributes for a machine image will depend on what applications you are using the "cattle" virtual machines for. However, you will almost definitely want to track the following:

- Is it a machine image or a block store?

- Is it a boot disk for an operating system, is it Windows, Linux, FreeBSD, NetBSD? And what version?

- Who is paying the bill for this to continue to be stored?

There will also be relationships, such as which application makes use of the block store or machine image.

5.3.8   Queues and other objects

Depending on which IaaS provided you use, there may be other functionality that your applications rely on. For example in the Amazon cloud it is very common to use the Simple Queue Service. If the loss of the queue would have an impact on your application and you have some way of monitoring the functionality of the queue (for example by putting synthetic transactions through it) then it makes sense to model the queue as a CI, and to record the dependency of your application on that CI.

Amazon search is another common service which applications depend on.

5.3.9   An example

In the following example, we have a shop front which has many images and other static content. We serve that static content from a bucket called s3://acme-shopfront-bucket/.

However we presumably update this bucket regularly whenever new products are added. There is a program called the Jobspawn Master which runs on a virtual machine in the Amazon cloud which has been given the hostname `jbspserv01.acme.com`. Given that it has a name, it's fairly likely to be a "pet" virtual machine. It runs in a security group along with the worker machines which do the writing into buckets from the master source of the shopfront information (not shown).

The worker machines boot up from a copy of the ACME popengine boot disk, and are entirely transitory, not using any kind of long-term data backing store. They retrieved jobs out of the queue for products to be updated. The queue is populated by the Jobspawn Master program.

This is the kind of diagram which would represent the CIs and their relationships.

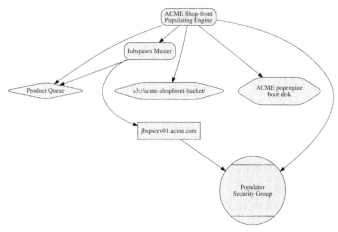

Chapter 6

About the author

Greg Baker works as a consultant and trainer with a wide spectrum of clients ranging from the very small to some of the world's largest. When he isn't writing books or consulting, he runs face-to-face training classes, develops e-learning and writes software.

Greg's email address is `gregb@ifost.org.au`. Write to him and tell him what you would like to see added to this book in the next edition, or any ideas you have for other books.

Made in the USA
Coppell, TX
22 January 2020

14892878R00039